BLAST OFF!

How Mary Sherman Morgan Fueled America into Space

Suzanne Slade

Illustrated by
Sally Wern Comport

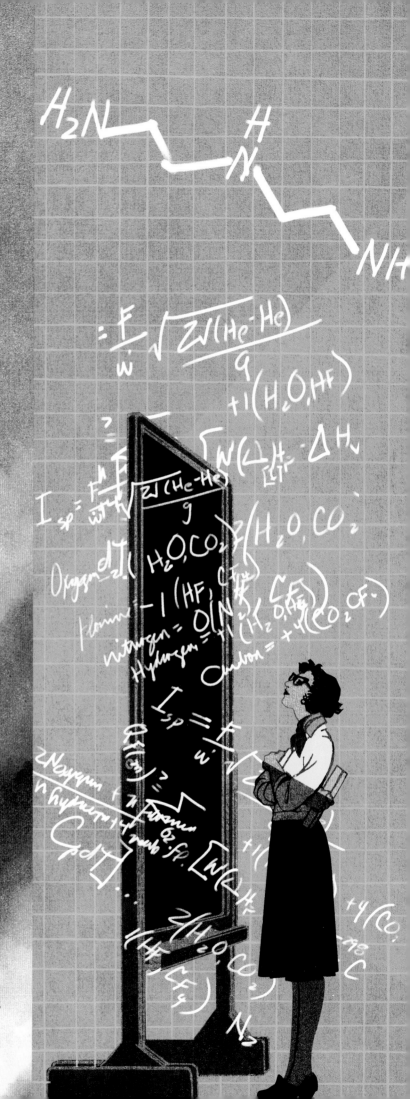

CALKINS CREEK

AN IMPRINT OF ASTRA BOOKS FOR YOUNG READERS

New York

Mary Sherman grew up on a farm in North Dakota with four older brothers and sisters. But there was always too much work for too few hands. Though women had been able to vote for nearly ten years, Mary couldn't vote about her chores. All day long she fed chickens, milked cows, and cleaned the creamer.

Until one day the sheriff and a social services woman came calling. They said eight-year-old Mary belonged in school. It was the law!

All the children at school knew how to read—except Mary. She didn't even know the alphabet. Mary worked hard to catch up, but she had to keep up with her chores too. While milking the cows, she studied the sound of each letter. Before long, she was reading stacks of books. Mary loved learning, and her favorite subject was science.

In high school Mary fell hopelessly in love with chemistry. She was fascinated by how tiny atoms made up everything—her desk, books, and even the twinkling stars.

Mary longed to study chemistry in college. But her parents wanted her home doing chores.

So, Mary devised a plan. She worked several jobs, applied for scholarships, and saved every penny. After graduating as valedictorian of her high school class, she hopped a bus bound for Ohio.

In her college chemistry class, Mary learned how atoms react with each other to create energy—heat and light. But after two years, Mary ran out of money and had to leave school.

A nearby lab called Plum Brook needed help making supplies for soldiers. Many of their chemists had left to serve in World War II. Mary landed a job at Plum Brook where she worked with chemicals that created powerful energy explosions!

Years later, the war ended. No war meant no job. Mary searched for a career where she could nurture her passion for chemistry.

Fortunately, a lab at North American Aviation in California was looking for chemists to design fuel for rockets—rockets that would explore space! To Mary, it sounded like the best job in the world.

But the ad said "college degree." Mary only had half a degree, but she knew she could do the work.

The man at the employment desk was surprised to see Mary. So were the men waiting to apply for jobs. But Mary didn't care how much they stared (or glared). She wasn't about to give up.

The engineering supervisor believed science was for men, not women. All nine hundred scientists in his department were men. Intent on proving him wrong, Mary handed him her résumé showing why she was the perfect candidate:

Top grades in college chemistry classes.

Three years' experience in a science lab.

Letters stating she was a hardworking chemist.

The man was baffled. Mary had the right qualifications. But she was a woman—a very determined woman!

He decided to take a chance. . . .

Mary was thrilled to be back in a lab. She studied how rocket fuels acted in different situations:
under pressure,
in hot and cold temperatures,
and mixed with other fuels.
Mary discovered each fuel had its own personality, just like her coworkers. Some were hotheads. Others were calm and stable. And some didn't mix well with others!

$y = -4E-07x + 0.0001x - 0.0132x + 0.679x +$

[km/h]

Using a slide rule, Mary made calculations that told her exactly how each fuel mixture would make a rocket fly—without launching a single rocket!

After years of hard work and experiments (and occasional explosions!), Mary became *the* rocket fuel expert.

MICROMETEOR GAUGES

SERGEANT ROCKET MOTOR

Explorer-I satellite.

One day Mary's lab received a top secret project: create the fuel to launch a rocket carrying America's first satellite into space. As it circled Earth, the satellite would collect information about space, like temperature and radiation levels. This would help engineers design future spacecraft for astronauts.

But this plan had a top secret problem. No one could find a fuel to make the rocket fly properly. Not even the rocket designer or his team.

The assignment was complicated. The engineering supervisor needed his "best man" for the job, but everyone knew the "best man" was Mary.

Mary bravely accepted the assignment. She couldn't wait to help America blast into space. She received two assistants. Both had engineering degrees, but no experience working with fuels. It was up to Mary to solve this colossal problem. If she didn't, America might give up on space exploration altogether!

First, she listed every rocket fuel—hydrazine, aniline, ethylene, and more. She needed one that was safe. Easy to get. Stable at high temperatures. And it had to create enough energy to push a rocket—*and* a satellite—into space.

Mary scribbled pages of computations. She pushed buttons on her mechanical calculator.

Some fuels created the right amount of heat, but not enough power.

Others produced the perfect power but weren't stable.

All the numbers said the same thing—none of the fuels would work!

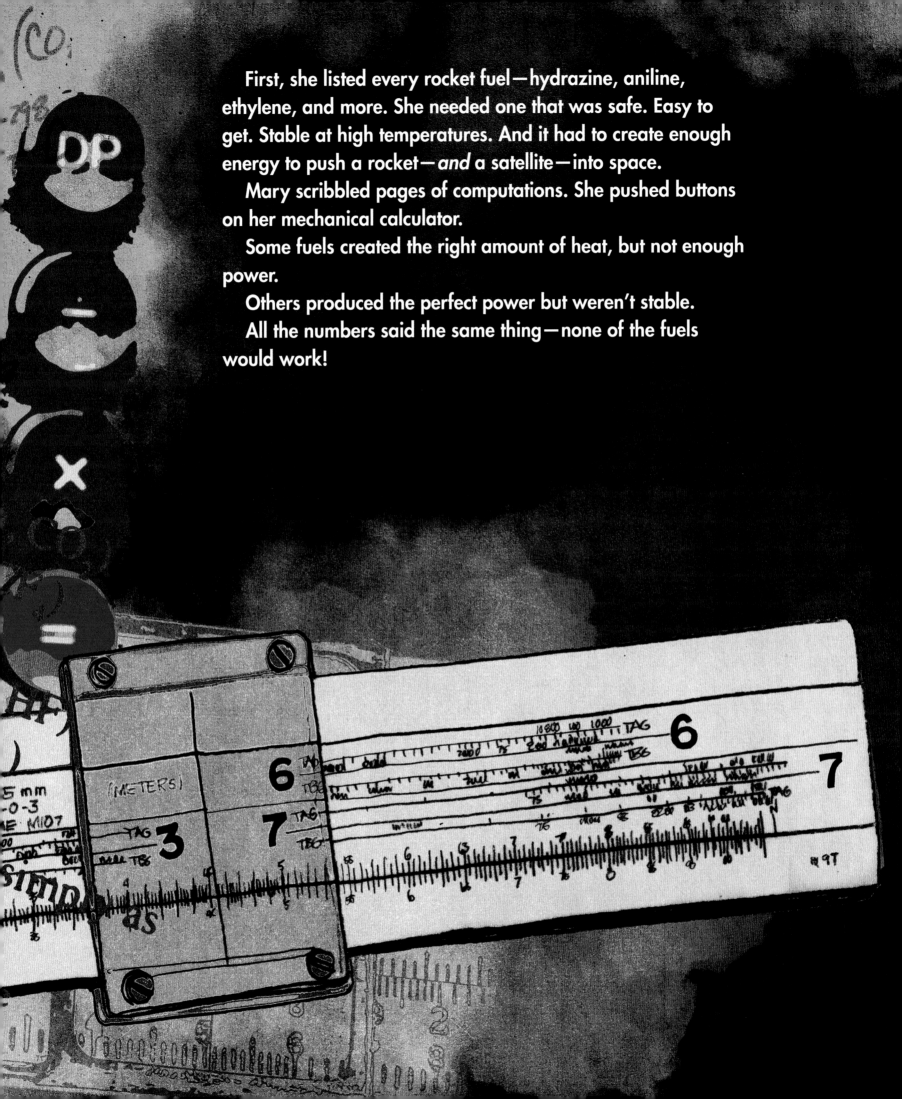

Mary had an idea. Could she mix two fuels
together to make something new?
    Her pen scratched out more calculations. Finally,
she found a mixture that worked—*on paper.*
    But how would it burn in a real rocket engine?

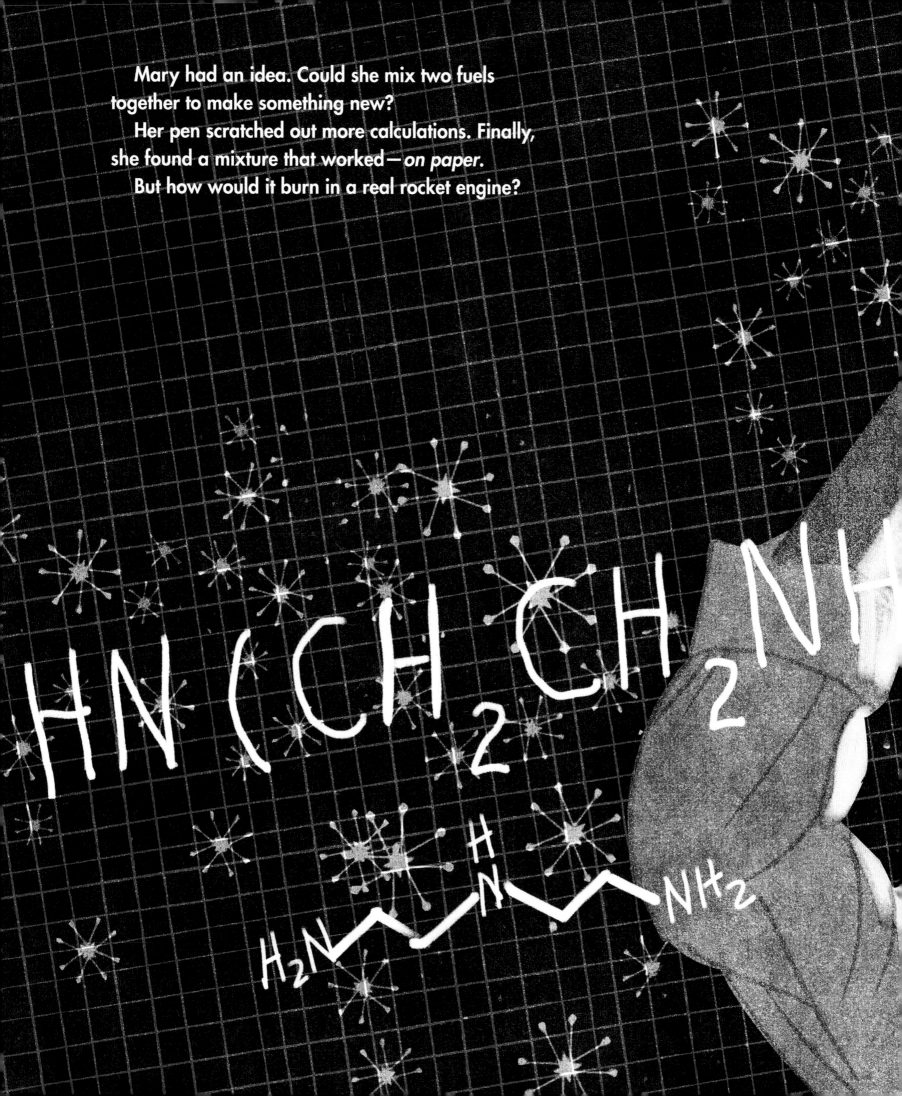

Mary ordered a batch of her fuel concoction called *hydyne*. Then she headed out to "the Hill," a secluded desert area. She needed to see how the fuel burned during an engine test on the ground.

Technicians poured her new fuel into an engine. Would it fire properly? Or ignite a deadly disaster? Mary and the team held their breath.

Soon the engine roared to life. The ground shuddered like a powerful earthquake.

Seconds later, the engine stopped!

Mary checked her numbers but didn't find any mistakes.

They began the test again.

The engine fired a second time. Then suddenly shut down.

Frustrated, Mary ordered a third test. But it failed too.

Mary returned to her lab. She poured piles of numbers into new computations.

She ordered more tests.

One by one, each failed.

Frustrated engineers, technicians, and scientists all looked for something or someone to blame. *The engine design isn't right! The fuel is wrong! Mary should be replaced with a man!*

Mary made more calculations. Engineers changed how the fuel flowed into the engine. Then everyone trudged back to the Hill.

As the engine ignited, Mary crossed her fingers. *If it didn't work, would people give up on the project?*
The engine roared . . . and kept roaring.

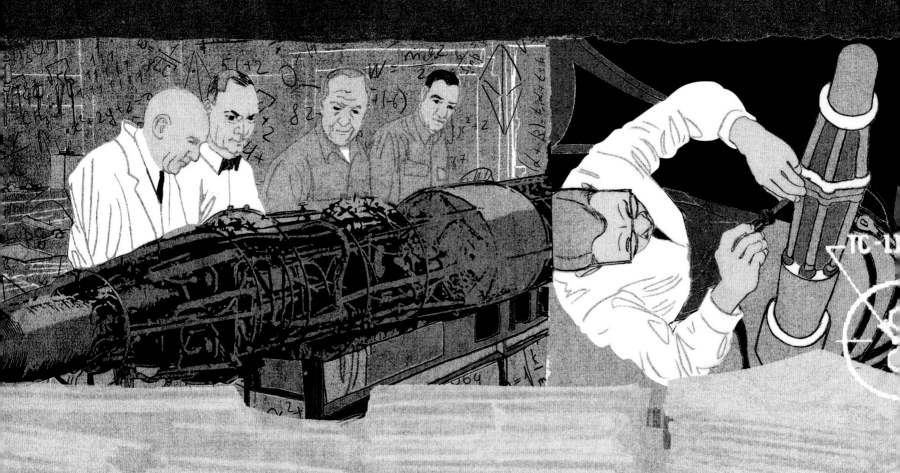

After two more successful tests, Mary's fuel was ready to fly!
But the project couldn't launch yet. Engineers had to prepare the
rocket and satellite for flight. Officials had to file the proper paperwork.
And the rocket designer needed to approve *everything*.

Meanwhile, navy engineers were furiously working on a different rocket that they hoped would launch America's first satellite into space.

On December 6, 1957, reporters anxiously watched as the navy's mighty Vanguard rocket lifted off. Two seconds later, it fell to the ground and exploded in a ball of fire!

The country was devastated. Many Americans decided space travel was too hard. Too expensive. And way too dangerous!

But not Mary. She knew exploring space would lead to important future discoveries.

Two months later (and more than two years after Mary first concocted hydyne!), technicians finally poured her fuel into a huge Juno I rocket. Stars sparkled in the night sky, while America silently worried: Will this be another launch disaster?

Mary held her trusty slide rule tight as the countdown began.

She knew numbers couldn't lie. And her pages of numbers said this rocket was going into space.

A hiss of white vapor swirled around the rocket.

The fuel ignited. *Liftoff!*

Flames spewed from the rocket as it slowly crawled
up the black sky.
　　Mary's fuel burned—smooth and steady—as it pushed
the rocket faster. Higher.

WEDNESDAY, 29 JANUARY 1958 --

1000 HRS ALL SET, BUT WEATHER BAD WITH HIGH
SURFACE AND UPPER WINDS. X HOUR IS
2230 +/- 2 HOURS. WILL WAIT FOR LATER
WEATHER BEFORE DECISION.

1330 HRS STILL ON X = 2230 +/- 2 HRS, BUT
WEATHER NOT IMPROVING.

1500 HRS X = 2230 + 2 HRS. WINDS NOT DECREASING.

1700 HRS NO CHANGE.

1900 HRS HOLD FOR TOMORROW, SAME X.

THURSDAY, 30 JANUARY 1958 --

0900 HRS NO CHANGE IN PLAN.

FRIDAY, 31 JANUARY 1958 --

1500 HRS STARTING COUNT DOWN, DECISION STILL
RESERVED.

1700 HRS LOOKS BETTER. X = 2230 + 2 HRS. THINK
WE'RE PROBABLY IN. VOICES BEGIN TO

2200 HRS X - 45 AND COUNTING. EVERYTHING STILL
GOING SMOOTHLY.

TOWER MOVES BACK - REPEATED ON RADIO

FLOODLIGHTS ON - " " "

PAD CLEARED - "

TOPPING OFF -

THE COUNT IS ON THE MINUTES N

X - 10, - 9, - 8, - 7, - 6,
- 1, ZERO!

IGNITI
IN GE
T (X + 15 SEC

$$\Delta v = v_e \ln \frac{m_0}{m_f} = I_{sp} g_0 \ln \frac{m_0}{m_f}$$

Then right on schedule, the rocket released America's first satellite into space. It began circling Earth, exploring the spectacular wonders of space.

Fueled by Mary's concoction, the groundbreaking mission inspired a nation.

And that was just the beginning!

DATES & DETAILS

August 1920—American women are given the right to vote.

November 4, 1921—Mary Sherman is born on the family farm in Ray, North Dakota.

1929—Mary starts school for the first time at age eight.

September 1, 1939—World War II begins.

May 31, 1940—At nineteen, Mary graduates from Ray High School as class valedictorian.

Summer 1940—Mary runs away from home to start college.

Fall 1940—Mary enrolls at DeSales College near Toledo, Ohio, as a chemistry major.

1943—Mary becomes a chemist at Plum Brook Ordnance Works near Sandusky, Ohio.

September 2, 1945—World War II ends.

July 15, 1947—Mary begins working in the Aerophysics Lab at North American Aviation in Inglewood, California.

July 29, 1951—Mary marries rocket engineer George Richard Morgan.

1953—Mary accepts a top secret assignment to design fuel for the Juno I rocket, which was slated to launch America's first satellite.

1953–55—Mary evaluates various fuel and oxidizers. She develops hydyne fuel.

December 1955—Mary retires from aerospace work.

October 4, 1957—The Soviet Union launches the world's first satellite, Sputnik, into Earth orbit.

December 6, 1957—The navy's Vanguard rocket attempts to launch America's first satellite, but it bursts into flames on a launchpad at Cape Canaveral, Florida.

January 31, 1958—Powered by Mary's hydyne fuel, the Juno I launches America's first satellite into Earth orbit. After reaching orbit, the satellite is named Explorer 1.

July 29, 1958—The National Aeronautics and Space Administration (NASA) is founded.

May 5, 1961—A Redstone rocket carries the first American astronaut, Alan Shepard, into space.

July 20, 1969—Neil Armstrong becomes the first human to walk on the moon.

March 31, 1970—After more than fifty-eight thousand orbits, Explorer 1 makes a fiery reentry into Earth's atmosphere and burns up.

January 1978—NASA begins accepting female candidates into the astronaut program.

November 2, 2000—The International Space Station welcomes its first crew.

August 4, 2004—Mary Sherman Morgan dies.

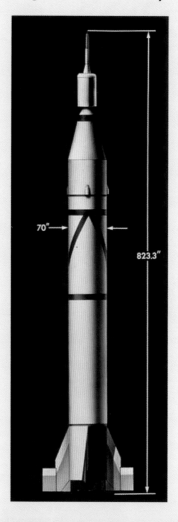

Juno I rocket that launched America's first satellite, Explorer 1, in 1958

MORE ABOUT MARY

Mary Sherman began working at North American Aviation (NAA) in 1947. As a theoretical performance specialist, she figured out how different fuels would perform in rocket engines when mixed with particular oxidizers (substances needed for fuels to burn). Her calculations predicted how a rocket would fly with various fuel-oxidizer combinations.

While working at NAA, Mary met a redheaded engineer named Richard Morgan. In his free time, Richard enjoyed playing bridge, just like Mary. Together they shared passions for science, space exploration, and cards. It didn't take long for the two to fall in love and marry.

After six years at NAA, Mary accepted an assignment on a top secret project to put America's first satellite in space. Finding a fuel and oxidizer combination that would propel the Juno I rocket high enough to place a satellite into orbit was a huge undertaking. Mary's assistants, Bill Webber and Toru Shimizu, had master's degrees in engineering. But they were fresh out of college with no real-world rocket or fuel experience. After many calculations and ground tests, Mary developed a fuel concoction of two liquid chemicals: unsymmetrical dimethylhydrazine and diethylenetriamine. Her fuel needed a name (hopefully one shorter than its ingredients), so Mary brainstormed ideas. The oxidizer she'd chosen to use with her fuel was liquid oxygen, or LOX for short. That got her thinking about a different lox—the salty salmon eaten on top of a bagel with cream cheese. Inspired by the "bagel and lox," she named her fuel Bagel. But Army officials wanted a more "scientific" name, so the fuel became known as *hydyne*.

In 1953 Mary and her husband welcomed a baby boy named George. A few years later, as Mary's due date for their second child drew near, she decided to leave the work she loved to stay home and raise her family. But she continued to closely follow America's accomplishments in space—including the Explorer 1 satellite launch, the Apollo moon landing missions, and the world's first astronauts working together on the International Space Station.

Mary Sherman's 1938 Ray High School (ND) class photo. She's in the third row, second from the right (dark top and glasses.)

EXPLORER 1

Surprisingly, America's first satellite didn't have a name when it soared into space on January 31, 1958. After it began orbiting Earth scientists decided to call it Explorer 1. It circled Earth about every 115 minutes (12.5 orbits a day). The satellite was 80 in. (203 cm) long, 6.25 in. (15.9 cm) in diameter, and weighed only 30.7 lb. (14 kg), but it sent lots of important data back to scientists.

Explorer 1 carried a cosmic ray detector that measured radiation in Earth orbit. This information helped scientists better understand the dangers future astronauts might encounter. The cosmic ray detector also discovered bands of highly charged particles around Earth that were later named the Van Allen radiation belts.

Equipped with five temperature sensors, Explorer 1 recorded temperatures in various locations of space. Engineers used this data to design future satellites and spacecraft that could keep working in extremely hot and cold conditions. Explorer 1 also carried detectors that recorded micrometeorite impacts, which helped scientists learn more about space and the solar system.

On May 23, 1958, Explorer 1 sent its final transmission before its batteries ran out. But it continued circling Earth for nearly twelve more years—a total of more than fifty-eight thousand orbits. The satellite reentered Earth's atmosphere on March 31, 1970, and burned up as expected.

The launch of Explorer 1 marked America's entry into the "space race" with the Soviet Union. Due to its success, more satellites were soon sent into orbit. Dozens of Explorer missions continued studying space, which helped scientists develop future spacecraft such as the rocket that carried Alan Shepard, the first American in space, in 1961. These early space flights paved the way for explorers to visit the moon, live on the International Space Station, and much more!

America's first satellite in space, Explorer 1

Explorer 1 is mounted on top of a rocket.

THE JUNO I ROCKET

A rocket called Juno I (a Jupiter-C rocket from the Redstone rocket family) launched America's first satellite into space. This seventy-foot rocket was designed by German American engineer Wernher von Braun. When von Braun's team discovered the rocket wouldn't be able to fly high enough to place Explorer 1 into Earth orbit, Mary and her fuel concoction came to the rescue. Mary's fuel was designed for the rocket's first stage, which pushed the rocket off the ground and into space.

The Juno I rocket lifted off from Cape Canaveral on January 31, 1958, at 10:48 p.m. The launch was originally scheduled for two days earlier, but strong Florida winds had caused a delay. The rocket soared more than two hundred miles before releasing Explorer 1 into space, where it began orbiting Earth.

As America celebrated this success, Wernher von Braun celebrated the woman who created the fuel that helped his rocket fly. He didn't even know her name, but he sent her a letter of gratitude which began, "Dear Unknown Lady." Though Mary's name was missing from the letter, and her legacy was missing from history for a long time, now many people know Mary Morgan and her valuable contribution to America's space program.

The Juno I rocket launches with the Explorer 1 satellite.

SELECTED BIBLIOGRAPHY

Bille, Matt, and Erika Lishock. *The First Space Race: Launching the World's First Satellites*. College Station: Texas A&M University Press, 2004.

Jackson, Libby. *Galaxy Girls: 50 Amazing Stories of Women in Space*. New York: Harper Design, 2018.

Lerner, Preston. "Soundings: She Put the High in Hydyne." *Air & Space*, March 2009: 10.

Lutz, Ota. "Explorer 1 Anniversary Marks 60 Years of Science in Space." January 12, 2018. jpl.nasa.gov/edu/news/2018/1/12/explorer-1-anniversary-marks-60-years-of-science-in-space.

Morgan, George D. *Rocket Girl: The Story of Mary Sherman Morgan, America's First Female Rocket Scientist*. Amherst, NY: Prometheus Books, 2013.

NASA.gov. "Explorer 1." December 18, 2007. nasa/mission_pages/explorer/explorer.html.

——. "Explorer 1 Overview." Last updated August 3, 2017. nasa.gov/mission_pages/explorer/explorer-overview.html.

——. "Explorer-I and Jupiter-C." history.nasa.gov/sputnik/expinfo.html.

——. "Stories of Missions Past: Early Explorers." October 26, 2011. nasa.gov/topics/history/features/explorer1.html.

O'Donnell, Franklin. *Explorer I*. Jet Propulsion Laboratory, California Institute of Technology: 2007.

AUTHOR'S NOTE

Of all my picture books, *Blast Off!* proved to be one of the most challenging to research. There are many reliable sources about Explorer 1, the Juno I rocket, and the Vanguard rocket launch failure; however, Mary Morgan's history is not well-documented. Unfortunately, this is true of many women who have made meaningful contributions to science and other fields. Early historians often ignored women because they believed their work was unimportant.

After hitting many research dead ends, I considered dropping the story. But I didn't want Mary to be another one of the groundbreaking women that history books overlooked. I was also personally drawn to Mary's story because of my interest in space exploration and my work at McDonnell Douglas Space Systems on Delta and Titan rockets and the Delta Star spacecraft (I have a mechanical engineering degree).

So, I decided to dig back into research and reached out to aerospace experts, helpful people in Ray, North Dakota (where Mary grew up), and Mary's son, George D. Morgan (who wrote a compelling book about his mother). Over time I uncovered the main facts of how Mary pursued her passion for chemistry and concocted a new fuel that launched America into space. Since certain details were impossible to find, I used known facts to creatively fill in a few gaps, which is why this book is historical fiction. I hope Mary's inspiring story encourages readers who face challenges because of their gender, background, or other reasons to continue pursuing their passions and dreams.

ACKNOWLEDGMENTS

Many thanks to the following experts for their generous help: Erik M. Conway, PhD, Jet Propulsion Laboratory (JPL) historian; Alan Buis, JPL; Bradley Rafferty, aerospace engineer; Carolyn Cowling; Carla Hodenfield, Ray (ND) Opera House Museum; Ashley Thronson, State Historical Society of North Dakota; Bernadette Purdue, Ray Public School; and George D. Morgan. And my deepest gratitude to my editor, Carolyn Yoder, for her insights and encouragement on the project.

Technicians and engineers monitor the countdown for the liftoff of Explorer 1 in the control room of the blockhouse at Space Launch Complex 26 at Cape Canaveral, Florida.

Dr. William Pickering, Dr. James Van Allen, and Dr. Wernher von Braun (left to right), hold up a model of Explorer 1 after its successful launch.

With love to my mother, who taught me that women belong in science —*SS*

In salute of Mary Morgan, your persistence and resilience in pursuit of an idea has fueled a future for young women's minds. —*SWC*

PICTURE CREDITS

Calkins Creek
An imprint of Astra Books for Young Readers, a division of Astra Publishing House
calkinscreekbooks.com

Printed in China

ISBN: 978-1-68437-241-6 (hc)
ISBN: 978-1-63592-559-3 (eBook)
Library of Congress Control Number: 2021906344

First edition
10 9 8 7 6 5 4 3 2 1

Design by Barbara Grzeslo
The text is set in Futura Std medium.
The illustrations are a hybrid of collage, digital collage, prisma drawings on vellum, and digital paint.